How to raise a plant and make it love you back.

**Morgan Doane and Erin Harding
of *House Plant Club***

How to raise a plant and make it love you back.

Laurence King Publishing

LAURENCE KING

Published in 2018
by Laurence King Publishing Ltd
361–373 City Road
London EC1V 1LR
Tel: +44 (0)20 7841 6900
Email: enquiries@laurenceking.com
www.laurenceking.com

Reprinted 2018, 2019 (three times), 2020 (3 times)

A catalog record for this book is
available from the British Library.

ISBN: 978-1-78627-302-4

Design: Masumi Briozzo
Copy editing: Jessica Spencer

Printed in China

Laurence King Publishing is committed to
ethical and sustainable production. We are
proud participants in The Book Chain Project ®
bookchainproject.com

The information and instructions about window
aspect are given throughout the book from
the point of view of the northern hemisphere;
readers in the southern hemisphere should
reverse them in order to get the best results.

Contents

Why we love plants

This book is the product of a cross-country plant friendship. A few years ago, we began independently documenting our daily plant musings with photographs on Instagram. We captured everything from how to drill a drainage hole in a thrifted coffee mug to the new leaf emerging on a *Monstera deliciosa*. We knew each other at first only as our Instagram usernames @cleverbloom (Erin) and @plantingpink (Morgan). We sealed our online friendship by trading plant cuttings in the mail. From Florida, Morgan sent a *Pilea peperomioides* to Erin. From Oregon, Erin returned the favor with a Chain of Hearts (*Ceropegia woodii*). Despite being about as far away from each other as we could be in the contiguous United States, our shared love for greenery grew. Eventually, that bond inspired us to create the online community House Plant Club, where people around the world share their plants with each other using the hashtag #houseplantclub.

Through House Plant Club, we have answered thousands of questions about plant care and identification, and it is in that vein that we decided to write this book. We believe raising plants can be an easy and rewarding hobby. Whether you are a seasoned green thumb with hundreds of houseplants or a newbie succulent lover with a thing for *Echeverias*, there's something in this book for you. We've filled it with our best tips and tricks, our very favorite plants, and some fun projects to try along the way. And, just as we were before this book, we're only a DM away over on Instagram if you get stuck trying to decide whether you brought home a *Philodendron* or *Epipremnum*.

While we've been actively sharing our plant passions online for only the past few years, we've both been "plant people" for decades and inherited that trait from the plant people who came before us. Neither of us is a botanist or biologist, but we know a thing or two about how to raise a houseplant and we've designed this book to walk you through how to do it too. We believe a house comes to life when you bring plants into it. Whether you want a few succulents on a windowsill or a bathroom full of *Begonias*, we will help you source, nurture, and propagate your plants so that they will love you back.

Erin and Morgan

GREEN UP
YOUR
SPACE

Let's go plant shopping! Whether online or in person at your local plant shop, be a savvy shopper. Learn how to assess your conditions before you bring home your new botanical beauties. That way, when you find yourself in a plant shop, you won't bring home something that wouldn't thrive in your space. Don't have an amazing plant shop in your area? Don't worry—online plant sellers offer just as much variety (if not more!), and you can shop from the comfort of your own home.

Consider your space before you shop

To set yourself up for success, consider your space before bringing a plant into it. It's heartbreaking to purchase the perfect plant only to bring it home and watch it waste away because it's not in an ideal environment.

Lighting
Evaluate your indoor lighting situation by determining which direction the available sunlight comes from. Also, consider light obstructions such as window treatments, houses, tall buildings, or fences. Knowing when your space is brightest and shadiest, as well as how far back into a room the sunlight reaches, will guide you in determining where to place your plants.

We live 3,000 miles apart from each other and we often talk about the weather and sunlight differences between Portland, Oregon, and Tampa, Florida. Depending on the season and where you live, different parts of the year can bring more or less intense sunlight. This will vary geographically, but it is another thing to consider when deciding where you can put plants in your home. In Florida, the winter sun shines directly into south-facing windows. Morgan moves her plants several feet farther away from the window to avoid the intense heat and direct rays. Erin's husband, Tim, made a wooden shelf for her hanging plants and it occupies a west-facing window that gets good light from the afternoon and evening sun.

East- and north-facing windows get more diffused sunlight so are typically best for low-light plants. The hospitable zone for these windows is smaller because less light comes in and spreads through the space. Because of this, you may need to use the windowsill, or a plant stand directly next to the window, to provide your plant with enough light. Succulents and cacti probably won't thrive in these spaces, but many plants can and will, including certain ivies, ferns, and snake plants.

Creating the ideal conditions

Use what you know about your space to select houseplants that will thrive in your conditions. If you don't have a lot of room, a plant that has a big footprint, like a *Monstera deliciosa,* might not be for you, but another plant in the same family, such as *Monstera adansonii,* can give you the same tropical vibe while remaining smaller. Succulents and cacti will put up with dry air, while tropical plants typically want things on the humid side. This isn't to say you can't keep a *Begonia* alive if you live in a dry place (because you may be able to supplement with a humidifier!), but if you can mimic a plant's natural environment it will be happier and healthier in the long run.

MONSTERA DELICIOSA

13

How to select happy houseplants

Once you find the perfect spot for a houseplant in your home, it's time to go shopping. So how do you decide where and when to purchase your greenery?

Where are you purchasing from?

First, consider the source. Dedicated plant shops, garden centers, and nurseries are staffed with people who work with plants full-time. Use them! They are often very knowledgeable about their charges. Other places to look for plants include farmers' markets, craft fairs, big-box stores, and even grocery stores.

If you are looking for a specific plant, bring a picture with you to the plant shop and ask a staff member if they have it in stock. Oftentimes, they can do a special order from one of their vendors if the plant you want isn't in the store. Otherwise, spend time in the plant shop and check out the different species and plant families they sell. Do they keep their succulents in good lighting? Are any of them stretching out from lack of sunshine? Can you tell if the plants have been maintained well? Check for dried, shriveled, crispy, or browning leaves. Avoid plants that aren't looking their best.

What to look out for

Once you find the plant you want, inspect it thoroughly. You'll quarantine it once you get it home, but it's better to leave an insect-y plant at the store than to bring it into your house and potentially infest your other plants. To look for pests, check the soil for movement and look at the stems and undersides of the leaves and the juncture between the leaves and stem. Check for tiny spiderwebs, as this is an indication of spider mites. Also look around the area where the plants are kept for tiny, slow fliers called fungus gnats. They live in the soil and can be hard to eradicate if you bring them home.

Asking for advice

Most plants will come with a tag with some identifying information and care tips. If you find a knowledgeable staff person at the store, ask them if they have any other advice. Take note of what kind of lighting the plant had while on display, keeping in mind that, given space restrictions in different stores, it may not have been in the ideal location. If you have to rely on the tag alone, don't trust it 100 per cent. In our experience, these tags are often vague or just plain wrong.

Transporting your new purchase

To avoid damaging plants while transporting them, use a cardboard box that won't tip over while you drive. Buckle it in, or wedge it against something heavy, so it won't tip or shift during your commute. If extreme weather shifts are an issue, consider wrapping the plant in plastic sheeting or newspaper for an added layer of protection. Don't leave plants in a hot car without air circulation, and avoid direct sunlight through the windows if you're traveling for any significant length of time. Try your best to keep the plant's surroundings as similar to its original environment as possible so it gets a good healthy start once you bring it home.

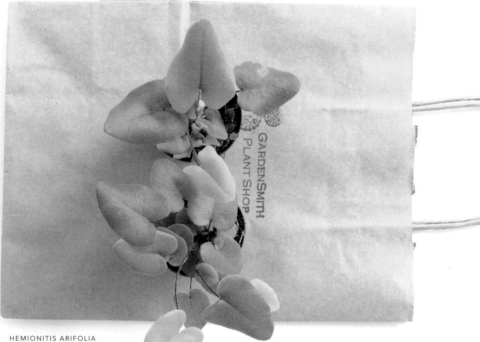

HEMIONITIS ARIFOLIA

Quarantining your plant

Even if you bring high-quality plants home from your favorite shop, keeping them separated from your existing plants at first isn't a bad idea. If you get cuttings from a friend or pick up a plant from somewhere you don't normally frequent, it's an even better idea to set them aside for an observation period. Choose a spot that is away from your other plants but that provides the new plant with adequate light and humidity. During this time, watch the plant for any signs of pests and treat them accordingly (see page 46 for more information on pest control). One week should give you enough time to identify any problems. If possible, during the quarantine period leave your new acquisition in whatever vessel it came in, so the plant doesn't endure the added stress of repotting.

Online plant shopping

We are both lucky to live in places with plenty of great, local plant shops. But not every area has a dedicated nursery with diverse foliage for sale. When your heart is set on a specific plant and you can't find it where you live, online vendors can often save the day. With the world wide web, almost any plant can be found (for a price!). Seasonal shipping restrictions, minimum order sizes, and shipping fees must all be factored in when buying online.

SCHLUMBERGERA
KALANCHOE THYRSIFLORA
ECHINOCEREUS REICHENBACHII
ECHEVERIA

Shipping a properly packaged plant can be expensive, especially if heat- or cold-packs are necessary to keep the plant's temperature regulated during transport. As with any online purchase, do your research by checking reviews or ratings, if available, before you buy. Unbox your purchase outside, or over newspaper, because soil often comes loose and can create a mess while unboxing. Vendors often include a care sheet that outlines how to revive your plant after its postal journey. Beyond these instructions, treat a mail-order plant just as you would one you found at a local shop by observing it for problems and abiding by a brief quarantine period.

HOYA CARNOSA 'CHELSEA'
SANSEVIERIA CYLINDRICA
PILEA PEPEROMIOIDES
EPIPREMNUM AUREUM

MAINTAINING
YOUR
COLLECTION

Plant maintenance doesn't have to be a full-time chore. Everything from propagation to repotting to vacation plant care can be broken down into an easy system. Once you have the basic routine down, you'll know how to pamper your plants so that they'll love you back. Keep the size of your plant collection to something you can manage. If a big plant becomes unruly, consider propagating it and giving the rooted cutting to a friend!

NEPHROLEPIS BISERRATA 'MACHO' / TRADESCANTIA FLUMINENSIS / SCINDAPSUS PICTUS / MONSTERA SILTEPECANA

Propagation

TRADESCANTIA FLUMINENSIS VARIEGATA
HOYA OBOVATA
SCINDAPSUS PICTUS
EPIPREMNUM AUREUM
MONSTERA SILTEPECANA
TRADESCANTIA FLUMINENSIS 'TRICOLOR'

Propagation is the act of creating a new plant from an existing one. It is a great way to multiply your collection and share plants with friends. There are many ways to propagate, but, with houseplants, the most common method is by rooting leaf or stem cuttings in water. Water propagation provides constant moisture that promotes root growth. Taking cuttings (also sometimes called clippings or starts) is a simple process, and most plants start to root within weeks. Not all plants can be rooted in water, but we've included a list of our favorites below.

While some people prefer to place their cuttings in soil immediately, it can be fun watching the roots form, and grow, in glass and water. Plants rooting in water make for great photographs, and the trend has caught on in home decor as well. Vintage glass jars, bud vases, and glass test-tubes can be made into propagation stations.

Our Favorite Plants to Root in Water

- *Pilea peperomioides*
- *Monstera adansonii* and *M. deliciosa*
- *Epipremnum aureum*
- *Tradescantia zebrina* and *T. fluminensis*
- *Philodendron*
- *Hoya*
- *Sansevieria*

TRADESCANTIA FLUMINENSIS 'TRICOLOR'

How to take a cutting

With a clean, sharp knife or scissors, cut a piece of stem approximately ¼ inch below a node. The node is the small bump, or area that holds the leaf buds, on the stem. Remove any leaves from the node area and place the cutting in clean, room-temperature water. Roots will form either from the end of the cutting or at the leaf nodes.

Care and maintenance

To increase your chances of success, take cuttings from strong, healthy plants. Provide them with bright, indirect light while rooting. All plants vary, but most will produce roots within a few weeks. Some leaf cuttings, such as *Ficus lyrata*, can take three months or more to root, while *Tradescantia zebrina* or *T. tricolor* send out roots within a few days. As long as the cutting is healthy and producing new growth, it can be left in water. Some plants, including *Epipremnum aureum*, can even be grown in water indefinitely. Keep the water level above the growing roots and replace the water once a week. Once the roots are long enough (about 4 to 6 inches), the cutting can be transferred to soil.

EPIPREMNUM AUREUM / SCINDAPSUS PICTUS

What to do with your new plants

Our favorite thing to do with rooted cuttings is to share them with friends. That's how our own friendship began! Owning plants with stories behind them makes them more special. Certain plants are highly coveted but only available regionally: shipping a rare plant to someone who can't find it locally is a sure way to seal a new friendship, as we can attest.

Sharing your cuttings
To prepare and package a cutting for shipping, soak a paper towel with water and gently wrap it around the roots of the plant. Enclose the roots and paper towel in a small plastic bag and use a twist tie to secure the top loosely. Carefully package it in a box by surrounding it with newspaper. Ship using the fastest method available, and instruct the recipient to put the cutting back in water to revive it after its journey.

Gifting your plant
Small potted plants also make perfect housewarming, teacher, or birthday gifts. Pot the plant and tie a bow around it for a quick and easy gift. To make it even more special, provide some accessories to go with the plant. Our favorites are macramé plant hangers, handmade ceramic pots, and small watering cans.

PHILODENDRON HEDERACEUM 'BRASIL' / PEPEROMIA CAPERATA

Boosting your original plant

Cuttings can also be used to make the original plant fuller. Poke holes in the soil and stick the rooted cuttings in the holes. Cover and press with soil to secure the roots. This can be done multiple times in order to achieve the desired fullness.

Documenting your plant

The process of propagating plants provides a perfect opportunity for photographing progression shots. These can be kept for your own reference, or shared with others in an online or in-person plant community. Online plant communities can be found on Instagram, Facebook, and other social-media outlets.

TRADESCANTIA FLUMINENSIS 'TRICOLOR'

Repotting and Potting Up

As plants age, their root systems either outgrow their current container or need a soil refresh to stay well fed. Repotting and potting up ensure the long-term health of your houseplants. The best time to follow these steps is right before plants enter their active growth spurt in spring.

Repotting

Selecting a vessel is the first step in the repotting process. Some plants (such as succulents and cacti) like to dry out and will do fine in clay pots, which are porous and help with water absorption and evaporation. Other plants, which need to retain more moisture, will do better in plastic. See page 41 for more information about plant containers. As for size, most plants need a pot with about 2 inches of room beyond the root system. Whichever vessel you choose, make sure it has a drainage hole for excess water to escape. This will allow you to water it freely without fear of root rot.

See page 42 for information about soil selection.

MONSTERA DELICIOSA
SYNGONIUM PODOPHYLLUM

Steps

1. Prepare your workspace by laying down newspaper or plastic sheeting. Cleaning up afterward will be much easier. Before removing a plant from its current container, gently massage the root area or tap it on a hard surface to loosen things up. Lightly pull on the main portion of the plant and slowly wiggle it from side to side until the plant is out safely. Use your hands to comb through the roots and loosen up the soil. Set the plant aside.

2. Fill the bottom 2 to 3 inches of the new pot with fresh soil. Next, place the plant inside the pot and continue to fill with soil around the edges. To avoid air pockets, pack the soil down lightly using your fingers. Now is the time to add top dressings, such as rocks or gravel, which can be aesthetically pleasing but also help with water retention. Lastly, water freshly potted plants thoroughly after repotting.

Potting up

Moving a plant you've had for a while into a larger pot is often called 'potting up'. In general, plants will exhibit clear signs of needing to be potted up, including:

· Exposed roots on top of the pot or poking out of the drainage hole
· Coiled roots filling a pot
· A plant in the same pot for a year or more
· Stunted growth on an otherwise healthy plant

Follow the steps for Repotting if you decide to pot up your plant to give it more room to grow. However, it may be the case that your plant does not need a bigger pot, but it would still benefit from fresh soil to restore nutrients. Gently remove the top inch or two of soil, mix with new soil, and replace, watering thoroughly.

MARANTA LEUCONEURA
SYNGONIUM PODOPHYLLUM

Vacation Plant Care

Several factors should be considered when deciding how to care for your plants while you are away from home. Depending on the type of plant, the time of year, and the length of time you'll be gone, different requirements need to be addressed. Of these, the time of year will be the biggest factor in determining just how much attention your plants need while you are away.

During spring and summer, temperatures are higher, days are longer, and plants are actively growing. They will need more water than in the winter, when they are resting and not putting out new leaves. If you're away in the winter, most plants will be fine with a thorough water prior to your departure and then a dry-out period while you are away. Some may start to wilt near the end of the week, but they should perk back up when you return with your watering can. Succulents and air plants will be the most forgiving during this hiatus. If you travel frequently, these may be your best bets.

If you are going away for a week in the summer, you will probably need to have a plant-sitter check in at least once, or use one of the vacation watering methods below. Before you go, test your desired method to see if it works for you!

Plant-sitter

If you are able to enlist the help of a friend or family member, provide them with a quick note about what needs to be done and when. Group plants with similar needs together before you go. Leave a full watering can next to your plants for easy access. Reward your plant-sitter with a cutting from one of your plants or a cute plant pot from wherever you've traveled.

ASPARAGUS RETROFRACTUS

Automatic watering devices

There are several types of vacation-watering tools available commercially. They all work similarly in that you fill a reservoir with water and insert it into the soil for a slow-release effect. Different sizes, materials, and methods are available. Terra-cotta stakes are perfect if you want to recycle a glass or plastic bottle. Simply fill the bottle with water, insert the bottle neck into the blunt end of the stake, invert, and push the stake into the soil. The terra-cotta will pull water from the bottle slowly and transfer it to the soil. For glass bulbs, add water directly to the stem, invert, and stick into your pot. These gadgets work best when inserted into pre-moistened soil.

EPIPREMNUM AUREUM
PEPEROMIA PUTEOLATA
PILEA PEPEROMIOIDES

The yarn trick

If you don't want to add more gadgets to your plant-care arsenal, you can make a DIY water-wick system with only a little counter space and a big jug of water. First, select a vessel that will hold enough water to sustain your plants while you're away. Fill it with water and assemble your plants around the vessel. Plants should be in pots with drainage holes and placed in a tray to catch any stray drops of water.

Next, cut enough pieces of yarn for each plant. The yarn should be long enough to hit the bottom of the large, water-filled vessel and have about 1 inch to nestle into the soil of each pot. Use a toothpick, or chopstick, to gently guide the yarn into the soil. Lastly, stretch the yarn from the plant pots up into the water reservoir. When each plant needs more water, it will pull from the reservoir through the yarn.

TOOLS, MATERIALS, AND TROUBLE-SHOOTING

Caring for plants doesn't require a vast toolbox full of equipment, but you might want to set aside a small space like a cupboard or work table for these essential plant-care items. You'll use them regularly to help keep your plants healthy and happy. The items we list here are important to have in your arsenal and come in various styles and price points, but inexpensive options often exist.

Tools of the Trade

PHILODENDRON 'CONGO'
NEMATANTHUS WETTSTEINII
MAMMILLARIA

Containers

Pairing plants with pots is one of the ways you can be creative with your collection. Let your personal style shine through with your container selections. Minimalists may want to stick with plain terra-cotta, or purchase all white, or all black containers for a monochromatic look. If you tend toward a more boho or eclectic vibe, mix terra-cotta with pots that feature bright colors, designs, and textures. For every home-design style, there is a complementary plant-container choice.

Plant containers come in many different materials, from fabric mesh to cement. Porous materials such as terra-cotta and stoneware absorb water from the soil. With these materials, more frequent watering may be required. Plastic pots aren't breathable, so they retain moisture longer. For this reason, you'll often find plants such as succulents and cacti in clay pots, and moisture-loving plants, such as ferns and *Begonias*, in plastic. The one overriding rule is that indoor-plant pots should have drainage holes, no matter what is planted inside.

Should you set your heart on a pot without drainage holes, don't fret. There are two ways to work with pots without drainage holes. First, you can drill drainage holes if you have a drill and diamond drill bit. Second, you can use the pot without holes as a cache pot. Cache pots are decorative outer containers that hide the plastic pot within. When watering, remove the plant from the cache pot and allow it to drain completely before putting it back in. Place a layer of rocks in the bottom of the cache pot to allow more air movement and to catch any last-minute drainage drips.

Soil

Each of the plants we highlight in our Plant Profiles section (see page 49) will do well with standard store-bought houseplant potting mix. We like standard mixes (not moisture-control) because they are light and airy, allow quick drainage and provide great starter nutrients for repotted plants. There are many brands of houseplant potting mix. Look for one that provides nutrients for up to six months, and scale back on any plant fertilizer you use at home until those six months are up. In addition to standard potting mix, it's handy to have a few amendments on hand to use as add-ins to the soil. These components provide extra aeration while helping to avoid common problems such as soggy or compacted soil.

Amendments

Perlite
Perlite is used to improve aeration in standard potting mixes. This white volcanic glass compound is light and airy, promoting healthy root growth by creating spaces within the soil and preventing compaction, which can suffocate roots.

Orchid bark
For houseplants with larger root systems, such as *Monstera deliciosa*, orchid bark can be used to increase airflow and prevent soil compaction. As a soil add-in, the looser consistency of orchid bark creates space for roots to grow and breathe in the soil.

Turface
Used to help absorb and retain excess moisture while providing space for drainage, turface is a light brown clay product. It is especially helpful as an additive for succulents and cacti. When the soil around the turface dries, it can pull moisture back out of the rocky clay granules.

Fertilizer

To stay happy and healthy, your houseplants will most likely need some plant food from time to time. It's important to know that standard houseplant potting mixes have enough nutrients to keep your plants fed for about six months after being repotted. After that, the plant will need to be fed to keep it looking great and growing well. There are several types of fertilizer available commercially, including granules, drops, and foam. Whichever type you choose, make sure to follow the package instructions carefully. Over-fertilizing can scorch plants and cause leaf loss. Fertilizer shouldn't be applied to unhealthy, immature, or dormant plants. In general, the larger and faster-growing a plant, the more nutrients it will need. Plants should be fed in spring and summer during active growth periods. We've made recommendations about fertilizer frequency in each of our plant profiles.

ORCHID BARK

TURFACE

PERLITE

POTTING SOIL

EPIPREMNUM AUREUM 'PEARLS AND JADE'

If space is a concern and you want only one watering can for both indoor and outdoor use, look for one that has a removable head. Detach the water-distribution head when using indoors to avoid pouring water far and wide. If plants are spread throughout your home, consider keeping different watering cans tucked among the different collections. The chore can seem much quicker if you refill the watering can after each watering session so it's ready to use the next time.

Watering cans

For all chores, but especially for watering plants, having the right tools can make all the difference. With no shortage of options picking a watering can will often come down to utilitarian or aesthetic preferences. Choosing the right watering can is about finding the balance between usefulness and style.

For indoor use, a watering can should have a narrow spout with a small pouring hole. A thin spout lets you maneuver the watering can within foliage so you can deliver the water directly to the soil. Save the watering cans with wide heads and many holes for outdoor use, where spreading water around a larger surface is more appropriate.

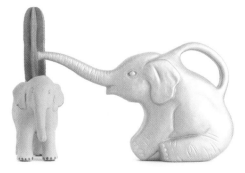

Aeration stick

Each time a plant is watered, the roots pull moisture from the wet soil. Over time, this can lead to soil compaction, which can cause root suffocation and, eventually, plant loss. To tell if the soil is compacted, observe how quickly water drains out of the pot. Dry, compacted soils tend to pull away from the pot so the water often runs right through down the sides.

Aeration prevents soil compaction by loosening things up and introducing air tunnels around the roots of the plant. In nature, organisms such as worms and burrowing bugs crawl through the soil around plants, providing much-needed oxygen to the root area. To simulate this at home, all you need is a chopstick (or similar sturdy stick) long enough to poke down into your plant pots.

To aerate, simply poke the stick into the plant's soil several times. If done regularly, there should be little resistance when inserting the stick. Follow up with your normal watering routine. For plants with heavily compacted soil, wet the soil first and then use the stick to loosen the root area by gently sticking it in and rocking it back and forth very slightly. Store the aeration stick next to the watering can or near your houseplants for easy access. Use it every other time you water to keep the soil aerated.

Tools

Having a few tools in your kit will come in handy when caring for houseplants. Whether you're repotting a plant, creating a terrarium, or inspecting for bugs, there is a tool for you. Small shovels and rakes (sold as terrarium tools) can be used to help you maneuver through the soil, while long tweezers make it easy for plants to be placed in small areas.

EPIPREMNUM AUREUM 'PEARLS AND JADE'
ECHINOPSIS PERUVIANA

Pest control

Dealing with plant pests can be broken down into three steps: detection, prevention, and eradication. We laid the foundation for detection and prevention earlier in the plant-shopping and quarantine sections. Unless you're experienced in insect eradication, don't buy a plant if you think it has pests, no matter how lovely it is; it's not worth potentially exposing your other plants to an infestation. During the quarantine period, keep an eye on your new acquisition to make sure nothing unsightly pops up after you bring the plant home. Should you find pests on a plant, knowing which type you're dealing with will help you decide the best way to proceed.

Prevention

Unhealthy plants are more susceptible to pests and disease. Preventing problems starts with providing adequate sunlight and just the right amount of water. Too much water leads to soggy soil and decaying roots, which some pests feed on. Too little sunlight and a plant will become weak. Sunlight can't penetrate fully through dust and debris, so keep leaves clean by washing them every so often. For large foliage, this can be done with a soft, damp cloth (much like dusting). For plants with more delicate foliage, carefully invert the plant into a bowl of water and swish the plant around gently. Tip the plant back over and allow it to drip dry after shaking off any excess moisture. Additionally, you can use systemic insect-control granules mixed into a plant's potting soil to deter pests chemically if you are so inclined.

Detection

When you water your plants, get up close and personal with them. Fungus gnats are often easiest to detect. They resemble fruit flies and live on the soil surface. They prefer overwatered soil and plants without top dressings, such as rocks. Above the soil, look at the tops and bottoms of leaves and focus on the spots where leaves and stems meet. This is a favorite hangout for spider mites. Their webs are very fine and the mites themselves are microscopic and hard to see. Sticky residue can be a sign of pests such as scale or aphids that excrete honeydew. Mealybugs look like small puffs of white cotton, and they typically congregate at stem junctures or where plants are juiciest. If you detect any of these pests on one plant, remove the plant from any shared space and look closely at any nearby plants for signs of spreading. Keep the affected plant(s) away from others until you've remedied the situation.

Eradication

If caught early enough, most pest problems can be fixed without chemical insecticides. Repotting may be the only way to get rid of a heavy fungus-gnat infestation. For other pests, use a drop or two of mild dish soap in a bowl of water and wipe affected areas down with a soft cloth. The same solution can be used in a spray bottle to loosen and dislodge pests such as scale, spider mites, and aphids. After spraying the area, go back over it with a clean cloth. Remove stubborn bugs with your fingernail or something small, like a toothpick. For mealybugs, dip a cotton swab in rubbing alcohol and apply it directly, then wipe off with a clean cloth. If a pest infestation is confined to one part of a plant, consider pruning that part off and disposing of it before it spreads. In extreme cases, it may be best to prune the plant heavily, or even throw it away. You may lose a plant that is cut back all the way to the soil, but it's better to start again with a healthy, non-infested one than to risk infecting everything else.

MONSTERA DELICIOSA

OUR FAVORITE PLANTS AND HOW TO CARE FOR THEM

Get ready to meet your new favorite greenery. These plant profiles feature some of the quirkiest, cutest, and quickest-growing varieties we have in our own homes. We focussed on plants that we've been successful with long term, and broke down how we care for them into 5 essential steps: Water, Light, Soil, Fertilizer, and Propagation. Because not all plants will work in every home, we tried to provide a nice assortment including small, medium, and large plants, as well as species that tolerate different levels of sunlight and maintenance.

Monstera deliciosa

Monstera deliciosa is a star among houseplants because of its striking leaf shapes and sizes. Its unique foliage is featured on many commercial products, from tea towels to coffee mugs. Nicknames for this plant include Swiss Cheese Plant and Fruit-salad Plant. It is also often erroneously referred to as Split-leaf Philodendron. Monstera is a separate genus from Philodendron, but they are similar in that they are both members of the Araceae family (the arums). Immature Monstera deliciosa plants have small heart-shaped leaves. More mature plants produce leaves with the signature holes and perforations.

Water
Water when the top inch of soil has dried out. Let the water run through the plant until it comes out of the drainage holes. Don't be afraid to set tropical plants such as *Monstera deliciosa* outside during a good rainstorm, or even in your shower stall, for a good soak.

Light
Native to rainforest environments, they are used to being shaded by taller trees. In the wild, they even use aerial roots to attach to trees and climb to great heights. In your home, you may need to provide your *Monstera deliciosa* with a surface that mimics a tree trunk, such as a moss pole (a stake or pipe covered with moss, readily available in stores and online) for the plant to climb. Place it in a bright spot without direct sun.

Soil
Standard potting soil can be amended with perlite for extra drainage and aeration, but it's not a must. Repot *Monstera deliciosa* every year in the spring to give its large root system fresh soil and nutrients. Container size does not necessarily need to increase every year as long as the roots all fit, with a bit of room left over in the pot.

Fertilizer
Standard houseplant fertilizer can be used, according to package directions, during the active growing season of spring and summer.

Propagation
Rooting *Monstera deliciosa* in water is easy and visually appealing. To propagate your plant, use a sharp knife to cut a stem off below a leaf

node. The main plant will also usually sprout a new leaf somewhere below the cut you made. Place the cutting in water, which you should change about once a week. Roots will begin to form after a few weeks. Once they reach 4 to 6 inches, it is safe to transfer the cutting to soil, in which it will continue to grow into a new plant.

Oxalis triangularis

Unique in coloring and in character, *Oxalis triangularis* brings a lot of color and movement to a houseplant collection—the leaves open during the day and fold in on themselves at night. These little gems, also known as Purple Shamrocks, grow from bulbs and are also popular landscaping plants. During the winter, the bulbs can remain dormant if kept cool and dry. New leaves will develop in the springtime. It's rare for flowers to bloom on other indoor plants, but *Oxalis triangularis* will produce small lilac-colored flowers while growing inside. *Oxalis* is a must-have for anyone looking for unique and colorful foliage.

OXALIS TRIANGULARIS BULBS

Water
Bulb-based plants can rot when overwatered, so allow the top inch or so of the soil to dry out each time before watering. Do not water during winter dormancy, but keep bulbs cool and dry. Start watering again in spring.

Light
Provide *Oxalis triangularis* with a well-lit spot away from direct sunlight. Outdoors it grows best in shady spaces, so work to simulate that in your home.

Soil

Oxalis triangularis prefers well-draining soil because of its bulbs. Amend standard houseplant potting mix with perlite for added drainage.

Fertilizer

Standard houseplant fertilizer can be used during the growing season. *Oxalis triangularis* will grow bigger and brighter when fertilized regularly.

Propagation

During dormancy, bulbs can be separated into sections and repotted in the same or separate pots.

Pilea peperomioides

What better way to begin a friendship than with a plant? A small *Pilea peperomioides* (also aptly known as the Pass-it-on Plant) traveled from Morgan's house in Florida to Erin's home in Oregon and the rest, as they say, is history. That once-small plant has now grown to produce its own offsets (daughter plants produced naturally from the mother) that, in turn, have been passed on to other plant lovers. *Pilea peperomioides* is easy to care for and produces plantlets so prolifically it's a joy to share. With its lily-pad-like leaves and quirky silhouette, it's a favorite of interior stylists and plant photographers. If you have one, you'll soon have many!

Water
A thirsty *Pilea peperomioides* will have droopy leaves. Water thoroughly about once a week, but in warmer climates or brighter sunlight, more frequent watering may be necessary. Use the soil as your guide—it should not be allowed to dry out completely, but also must not be left soggy.

Light
The key to a beautiful *Pilea peperomioides* is bright, indirect sunlight. A south- or west-facing window is ideal. These plants grow quickly toward the sunlight so, to ensure uniform growth, rotate the pot weekly. This will create a more well-rounded appearance.

Soil

Standard potting mix is fine for the Pass-it-on Plant, but it can be amended with add-ins such as orchid bark or perlite for extra air space and drainage. Sometimes "root babies" pop up in the soil, so this isn't the plant to top dress with rocks as you might succulents or cacti.

Fertilizer

Standard houseplant fertilizer can be used, according to package directions, during the active growing season of spring and summer.

Propagation

Use a clean, sharp knife to excise offsets from the main branch or as they pop up out of the soil. Offsets root best in water, but can also be planted directly into moist soil. Roots should form within weeks.

Tradescantia fluminensis 'Tricolor'

Tradescantia fluminensis 'Tricolor' is just as easy to care for as its more popular relative in the Wandering Jew family, *Tradescantia zebrina*. While *T. zebrina* sports purple leaves with silver and green markings, *T. fluminensis* features leaves that are green, pink, and cream. Considered to be invasive species in many places where they grow in the wild, *T. fluminensis* are hardy and fast-growing when kept as houseplants. In fact, they grow so quickly that they often become long and "leggy." Long, trailing stems can be snipped off to promote bushier growth for a more compact look.

Water

Not a particularly thirsty plant, *T. fluminensis* will put up with a bit of neglect. The more sunlight it receives, the more water it will need. *T. fluminensis* leaves stand up straight and orient toward the light when healthy. They'll begin to point downward and droop when it's time to top up with water.

Light

Variegated plants with lighter-colored leaves often require more light than their darker counterparts and *T. fluminensis* is no exception. This plant thrives in very bright light and can withstand direct sun through a window for a few hours a day. Adjust the watering schedule accordingly.

Soil

Standard houseplant mix is perfect for this unfussy plant. No amendments necessary.

Fertilizer

One or two fertilizer applications a year should be plenty for such an easy-going plant. *T. fluminensis* plants grow so quickly on their own, they don't need much encouragement.

Propagation

As *T. fluminensis* plants grow so fast, they can quickly become large and unruly. Snip off long stems, remove the lowest leaves, and place in water. Roots form on *T. fluminensis* cuttings quicker than on any other plant we've propagated, sometimes within just two days! They are also quick to fade in water, so, once the roots reach 1 inch, transfer back to potting mix and watch the cycle begin all over again.

Ficus lyrata

Ficus lyrata, **popularly known as Fiddle-leaf Fig, is one of the most popular houseplants of recent times. Almost every decor magazine, designer, and interior blogger has featured a Fiddle-leaf Fig at one time. With its large fiddle-shaped leaves, it's the perfect statement plant in any home. Despite its beauty, many people have a difficult time with *Ficus lyrata*. The key is to find a good spot for it and let it be. It doesn't like drafts, and prefers not to be moved. While it can be a finicky plant, with proper care and ideal conditions, the Fiddle-leaf Fig can be a showstopper.**

Water
Watering a Fiddle-leaf Fig can be tricky. The amount of water depends on the amount of light the plant is getting. We've found that giving it a thorough watering when the top few inches are dry is best. Be sure to remove excess water from the tray as soon as the water has finished draining. These plants do not enjoy being overwatered. A thirsty Fiddle-leaf Fig will have droopy leaves. If you see the signs, it's time to water.

Light
Bright, indirect light is best for *Ficus lyrata*. It will begin to grow toward the light, so rotating the plant will be necessary if you want it to grow uniformly. Wipe its leaves with a damp cloth once a week to remove dirt and dust. This will allow the plant to soak up as much light as possible.

Soil
Quick-draining indoor potting soil will work well for a Fiddle-leaf Fig. Adding perlite can promote good root growth by giving the roots space to move.

Fertilizer
Use fertilizer as directed in the spring and summer. Fertilizer will help *Ficus lyrata* grow strong and will promote larger leaf growth.

Propagation
Ficus lyrata can be easily propagated by cuttings. Cut a piece of stem from the top with three to four leaves attached. Place the cutting in water and wait for roots to grow. When roots reach 4 to 6 inches you can safely place the rooted plant in soil.

Philodendron

Philodendrons are some of the most commonly used houseplants for decorating. There are hundreds of species with varying shapes and colors, including silver, white, yellow, and even pink. Some *Philodendrons* are vining and look lovely in a hanging basket, or will grow upward with help from a moss pole. Others are non-vining: each individual leaf grows from the center of the plant. They are beautiful, easy-to-care-for plants, perfect for a beginner plant parent.

Water
Most *Philodendron* species have similar water needs. Water thoroughly when the top few inches of soil is dry. *Philodendrons* can stay slightly wet but not soggy. Leaves will start to droop or curl under when they need to be watered.

Light
In the wild, *Philodendrons* grow under towering trees, which protect them from direct sunlight. Mimicking their outdoor environment in your home can be done by placing them in a south- or west-facing window with a sheer curtain. This protects them from direct rays but they still get plenty of light.

Soil
Standard indoor potting soil will work just fine for *Philodendron* species. Aerate soil with a skewer when the soil becomes too compacted to allow roots to absorb water properly. Repot *Philodendrons* about once a year, when the roots start to coil tightly and grow out of the drainage hole.

Fertilizer
Use standard houseplant fertilizer, as directed, every few weeks in spring and summer.

Propagation

Philodendrons can be very easily propagated by stem cuttings. With a clean, sharp knife cut a stem, with two or three leaves, just below a node. Place the cutting in water and wait for roots to grow. When the roots are 4–6 inches long, pot your cutting in soil.

Succulents

Succulent plants are so named because they have plump, fleshy leaves that store water. They are great entry-level plants for someone looking for low-maintenance greenery. The wide variety of shapes, colors, and sizes of succulents makes collecting them endlessly exciting. From the trailing varieties such as *Sedum morganianum* (Burro's Tail) to the strange "living rocks" called *Lithops*, succulents provide quirkiness and character to any houseplant grouping. Although diverse in looks, most succulent plants prefer to be handled the same way, with bright light, well-draining soil, and not too much water.

Popular succulents to try

- *Aloe*
- *Ceropegia* (including Chain of Hearts)
- *Crassula* (including Jade Plants)
- *Echeveria*
- *Euphorbia*
- *Haworthia*
- *Kalanchoe*
- *Sedum*
- *Sempervivum*
- *Senecio* (including String of Pearls)

Water

During the growing season (spring and summer), succulents can be treated much like other houseplants. Water thoroughly once the top inch of soil has dried out. This can be done once a week or more, depending on the conditions of sunlight and heat. During winter, succulents need a rest period and should be watered only once or twice a month. Misting is not necessary for succulents—they do not benefit from added humidity.

Light

With few exceptions, succulent plants need direct sun daily in order to thrive. A south-facing windowsill is the ideal location for succulents indoors. Haworthia is a subset of succulents that will thrive without direct sun but should still be grown in bright, indirect light.

Soil

Drainage is key for succulents, as these plants do not do well when kept too wet. Turface is a great soil amendment and works well as a decorative top dressing, too. Specially formulated cactus and succulent soil is available commercially as an easy alternative to mixing and measuring your own.

Fertilizer

Succulents will grow fuller, and produce bigger and brighter blooms, when nourished properly. Standard houseplant fertilizer should be diluted slightly with water, to prevent scorching, and used about once a month during spring and summer. Specially formulated succulent fertilizers are available commercially as well.

Propagation

Propagating succulents has become a popular hobby among plant enthusiasts because it's very easy to do and requires little work. Almost any part of a succulent can become a new plant, whether stem or leaf cuttings. Some succulents produce offsets, which can be separated to become new plants. While other plant cuttings need to go directly into soil or water, succulent cuttings need a few days to dry out between separation and planting. Once the cut portion has callused over, it can be placed in succulent soil and watered lightly.

SEDUM MORGANIANUM
HAWORTHIA
SENECIO ROWLEYANUS
ECHEVERIA

Cacti

As houseplants, cacti provide great architectural detail. Some, such as *Cereus*, are tall and columnar, some are squat and round, like *Mammillaria*, and others are wide and branched, like *Opuntia*. Their hairs, hooks, spikes, and spines give them a defensive texture that you'll want to avoid, in case you get poked. If kept in the right conditions, some indoor cacti will bloom beautifully in the spring, which can be a rewarding surprise after a winter of neglect.

Water
Like succulents, cacti require winter rest periods when you can virtually ignore them. During this time water only once or twice a month, just enough so that they won't shrivel. Increase water in spring as the weather warms. During the active growing period, cacti can be watered similarly to other indoor plants. Once the top inch or so of soil has dried out, water thoroughly until the excess comes out of the drainage hole.

Light
Cacti should be kept year-round in the brightest light possible, with direct sunlight if available. South-facing windows will provide the best light. West-facing windows may suffice depending on your location, but north- and east-facing windows should be avoided.

Soil
Use fast-draining soil that won't hold on to moisture. Amend standard houseplant soil with turface or similar granules, or use commercially available soil specially formulated for succulents and cacti. Cacti do not need large containers in order to thrive.

Fertilizer
Treat like succulents. Dilute standard houseplant fertilizer and scale back recommended dosage by half. Do not fertilize during the winter rest period.

Propagation
Thick gloves are recommended whenever handling cacti. Propagate by taking stem cuttings or by removing branches or offsets. All cuttings should be allowed to dry out for a few days before placing in soil to form roots.

MAMMILLARIA RUESTII
FEROCACTUS EMORYI
MAMMILLARIA SPINOSISSIMA
MAMMILLARIA SCHIEDEANA

Sansevieria

The *Sansevieria* genus has over 70 different species. They come in many shapes and sizes, from long, thick, snakelike leaves to small, compact rosette shapes. With the varying colors of green, white, and yellow, this plant is perfect for any room in your home. Commonly known as Snake Plants, they are low-maintenance and regarded as some of the most indestructible plants, owing to their ability to adapt to almost any environment. When given ideal living conditions, *Sansevierias* can delight you by flowering.

Water
The most common cause of death in Snake Plants is overwatering (which causes root rot). Their thick leaves will store water for a long time, so watering is necessary only when the soil has completely dried out. When the soil is dry, water thoroughly until water runs out of the drainage holes. Be sure to remove any excess water from the saucer immediately.

Light
Sansevieria grow best in bright, indirect light. A south- or west-facing window with a sheer curtain would be an ideal indoor spot. They will tolerate low-light conditions, but will not thrive.

Soil
Snake Plants need fast-draining potting soil with a drainage hole in the pot. Plant your Snake in a terra-cotta pot using a cactus or succulent soil mixture. Alternatively, you could add amendments such as perlite or orchid bark to a regular indoor potting mix to provide better drainage.

Fertilizer

Indoor plant fertilizer can be used, as directed, once or twice in the spring and summer.

Propagation

There are a few ways of propagating *Sansevieria*. They can be grown from seeds and propagated from leaf cuttings, but the most common way is to separate offsets from the main plant. Small offsets grow from the mother plant through horizontal stems under the soil called rhizomes. Remove the whole plant from the pot and lay it on a piece of newspaper. With a clean, sharp knife, make a cut in the middle of the rhizome. Place the new plant in a pot of fresh potting soil and care for it as directed above. Place the mother plant back in its original pot.

SANSEVIERIA TRIFASCIATA
SANSEVIERIA 'FERNWOOD'

Hoya

Hoyas are beautiful flowering plants. Commonly referred to as Wax Plant or Wax Flower, these succulent-type plants come in many variations. *Hoya* leaves can be round, long and linear, or even heart-shaped. Small star-shaped flowers bloom and cluster in umbrella-like domes. The flowers vary in color and are quite sweet-smelling. *Hoyas* are epiphytic (able to grow without soil on other plants or objects) and structurally interesting, which makes them perfect mounted plants (see page 82, Mounts).

Water

Hoya leaves are able to store water for long periods. Be careful not to overwater them, as they prefer to be on the dry side. When the soil is nearly dry, water thoroughly until the water flows out of the drainage hole. Remove excess water from the saucer immediately. *Hoya* leaves will become soft and limp when they are thirsty. In the winter, allow the soil to dry out almost completely before watering.

Light

Hoyas need bright, indirect light. They are not low-light plants, so be sure you have proper light before bringing a *Hoya* home with you. A south-facing window with a sheer curtain would be an ideal location.

Soil

In their natural habitat, *Hoyas* can be found growing on trees. Their roots grow between and on top of tree bark, which gives them the air and space they need. Give them well-drained soil by adding perlite and orchid bark to the potting-soil mix. This will give their roots the space they need to grow strong and healthy. *Hoyas* like to be root-bound, so repotting is necessary only when the roots are coiled and growing out of the container.

Fertilizer

Fertilize *Hoyas* during active growing periods, every four to six weeks in spring and summer.

Propagation

Hoyas can be propagated easily by stem cuttings. With a clean, sharp knife or scissors, cut a piece of stem about 6–10 inches long. Break off the leaves closest to the bottom (where the stem was cut) and place the cutting in a cup of room-temperature water. Once the roots have grown approximately 4–6 inches long, the cutting can be planted in soil.

HOYA OBOVATA
HOYA CARNOSA 'TRICOLOR'
HOYA CARNOSA 'CHELSEA'

Chlorophytum comosum

Chlorophytum comosum is a flowering plant with long, slim leaves that resemble spider legs. Commonly referred to as Spider Plants, *Chlorophytum comosum* are easy-to-care-for plants that make a perfect first houseplant. Mature Spider Plants produce small, white flowers that bloom on long, branch-like stems. Baby Spider Plants grow at the ends of the branches and will produce their own roots when placed in water. A large *Chlorophytum comosum* looks beautiful in a hanging basket, and makes a perfect statement plant.

Water

Spider Plants need to be thoroughly watered as soon as the soil becomes dry. It is important that they have good drainage and that you don't overwater, as they can be susceptible to root rot. It is common for *Chlorophytum comosum* to develop brown tips. This is not a cause for concern. The brown tips are caused by fluoride in the water. To prevent them, use distilled water or rainwater for your plants.

Light

Chlorophytum comosum do very well in bright, indirect light. Plants placed in direct sunlight will begin to fade. To prevent this, use a sheer curtain in front of a south- or west-facing window. Spider Plants can also tolerate lower light levels (but will need to be watered less).

Soil

Spider Plants aren't fussy and will grow in almost any soil. Amendments such as perlite, turface or orchid bark can be added to improve drainage. Spider Plants prefer to be root-bound. Repot when you can see that the roots are coiled tightly, or when you notice the roots poking out of the drainage holes.

Fertilizer

Use liquid fertilizer for houseplants. Fertilize every four to six weeks in the spring and summer, when the plant is actively growing.

Propagation

Gently pluck the baby Spider Plants from the branch and place in a cup of water. Be sure water is covering the bottom of the plant at all times. Once the roots have developed, you can plant the baby Spider Plant in soil.

Epipremnum aureum

Most commonly referred to as Pothos or Devil's Ivy, this plant and its many cultivars are widely available at nurseries, plant shops, and even home-improvement stores. Cultivars are plants that have been selectively bred in cultivation. Golden Pothos, Marble Queen, and Pearls and Jade are all cultivars of *Epipremnum aureum*. Their leaves can be variegated, marbled white, or even green and golden. Each type is unique, but they all share similar care instructions. They are easy to tend and can adapt to different environments. Pothos can often be found in malls, bathrooms, and office cubicles owing to their ability to grow in low light. They grow quickly and will drape beautifully in hanging baskets or climb nicely up moss poles.

Water

Water *Epipremnum aureum* when the top few inches of soil becomes dry. Water evenly over the soil until the water starts to flow out of the drainage hole. Do not let the soil dry out completely.

Light

Epipremnum aureum does best in bright, indirect light. Cultivars with white, or light yellow, marbling will need the most light in order to maintain their variegation. If variegated plants don't get enough light (energy), they can lose variegation in new growth. On the other hand, some *Epipremnum aureum* plants can still grow nicely in low light.

Soil

Regular indoor potting soil works just fine for this plant. Choose one with added perlite (or add your own) to help promote air movement and root growth. Repot *Epipremnum aureum* every year, as needed. If the plant does not need to be repotted, you can add a layer of new soil to the top of the pot. This will replenish nutrients to the plant.

Fertilizer

It's not necessary to fertilize *Epipremnum aureum* very often, since it's a fast grower even without added nutrients. Feeding with standard indoor plant food once or twice a year should suffice.

Propagation

Epipremnum aureum is very easily propagated. Cuttings can be taken below a leaf node and placed in water to root. These can be left to grow in water indefinitely, or replanted in soil once the roots reach 4–6 inches. These plants are great to use in and around aquariums. They will take root in the water and can help to filter out toxins.

Tillandsia

Tillandsia are flowering plants in the Bromeliaceae family. Commonly referred to as Air Plants, these beautiful plants have the ability to live without soil. Most *Tillandsia* are epiphytes, which means they can grow on the surface of other plants or trees and pull nutrients from sources around them. They can be found in deserts, mountains, and forests, but acclimate well to homes, where they make fairly easy-to-care-for houseplants. Products such as frames, stands, and clips can be purchased to display *Tillandsia*. Or you can create your own fun hanging display using driftwood and thread!

Water

Fill a clean bowl with water and soak the *Tillandsia* in it for ten to fifteen minutes. Lift the plants out of the water and shake off the excess. Lay the *Tillandsia* on a towel upside down to allow any additional water to escape the inside of the plants. Once the plants are dry to the touch, they can be safely placed back in their display space or windowsill without fear of mold or rot. How often you water them depends on the amount of light they receive. Over time, you will get to know your plants and be able to recognize the signs of thirst. For *Tillandsia*, the tips may start to curl or the whole plant may start to feel crunchy. You can also spritz your plants with water in between soaking sessions if they look a little thirsty.

Light

Light is very important in relation to how much water your *Tillandsia* will require. They need bright indirect light and can also take direct sun in small doses. Housing *Tillandsia* on or near a windowsill can ensure they get enough light.

Soil

Tillandsia are popular decor plants because they don't require any soil to survive.

Fertilizer

Tillandsia fertilizers can be used to promote flower growth. Pre-mixed spray bottles or powder that can be mixed into soaking water can be purchased online and at many plant shops.

Propagation

Tillandsia sprout offsets or "pups" from the mother plant. When the pups reach one quarter to one third the size of the mother plant, the pups can be separated off. Gently pry the pups away from the mother plant with your hands. Once they are separated, follow the regular *Tillandsia* care instructions.

DIY PROJECTS

Having plants throughout your home means you'll need places to hang, display, and highlight them. Use these fun and easy Do It Yourself projects to create one-of-a-kind pieces that you'd never find on the shelf at a home decor store. Plus, you can tailor each project to your own specific style and space requirements. Invite some friends over and have a plant-filled craft session! These projects also make great gifts.

Mounts

Mounting a plant is a fun and easy way to bring a bit of green into your home. Short on surface space for your plants? Mounted plants are a perfect solution. These pieces of living art fit just about any style, from modern minimal to boho chic. With just a few supplies from your local or online nursery, you can make a mounted plant in no time.

Before you begin
The size of the plant should suit the size of the board. If you know the exact plant you are going to use, select a mounting board that complements the size of the plant. Alternatively, if you found the perfect mounting board, use it to inspire your plant selection.

Supplies

- Preserved Sheet Moss (responsibly sourced)
- Cup of water
- Scissors, pencil, hammer
- Florist's wire or fishing line
- Wall-hanging kit
- Mounting Board
  Suggestions: cedar fence-board, cork bark, driftwood
- Plant to mount
  Suggestions: *Hoya, Rhipsalis, Philodendron*
- Small clout nails (short body, big head)

RHIPSALIS LINDBERGIANA
LEPISMIUM CRUCIFORM
HOYA OBOVATA

Steps

1. Soak the moss in a cup of water for a few minutes.
2. Cut 3–4 feet of florist's wire or fishing line and set aside.
3. Attach the wall hanger to the back of the mounting board according to package instructions.
4. Remove the plant from its pot, leaving some soil attached to the roots.
5. Wrap the roots of the plant in the damp moss and position it on the board.
6. Trace a circle around the moss ball. Set the plant aside.
7. Hammer 6–12 nails to the front of the board, around the circle.
8. Choose any nail and securely knot one end of the fishing line or wire to the nail.
9. Place the plant in the middle of the circle.
10. Criss-cross the wire over the moss, back and forth from nail to nail, being sure to wrap it around the head of each successive nail.
11. Once the plant is secure, tie the wire to the final nail with a knot and cut off the excess.

Care and Maintenance

· Plants from the suggested list require bright, indirect light.
· To water, submerge the board, past the roots, in a tub of room-temperature water for approximately 30 minutes. Let the board drip dry before hanging it back on the wall. Repeat as necessary when the moss is no longer moist. Keep in mind that mounted plants will need to be watered more often than potted plants.
· Prune the plant as needed by trimming off old growth or yellowing leaves.
· Use the same steps to re-mount the plant to a bigger piece of wood as it grows.

Terrariums

Terrariums are self-contained ecosystems made up of soil, rocks, sand, plants, and more. They are perfect for people with limited space, since the plants can grow only as big as the container. Minimal maintenance is required, so terrariums are also great for those who travel or simply don't have the time to care for plants. Follow these easy steps to design your very own terrarium. It will make a lovely addition to any home or office.

Before you begin

The materials you need will be determined by the size of your container. When adding layers of material, keep in mind that there will be up to four layers of essential ingredients even before the plants are added. Be sure to leave enough room between the plants and the top of the terrarium. You will be able to plant one small plant every 2–3 inches, so, if your container is 5 inches in diameter, you can safely use two small plants. Not all plants will take to their new environment. If plants brown or die, remove and replace them immediately.

HEMIONITIS ARIFOLIA
CRYPTANTHUS 'PINK STAR'
PILEA CADIEREI
SAINTPAULIA
ATHYRIUM FILIX-FEMINA 'MINUTISSIMUM'

Supplies

- Glass container with cork or sealable lid

- Red lava rock

- Funnel (optional)

- Activated charcoal

- Indoor potting soil

- Decorative sand (optional)

- Small tropical plants and mosses
  <u>Suggestions</u>: Ferns, Orchids, African Violets, *Peperomia*, *Fittonia*, *Philodendron*, *Hypoestes*, *Croton*, *Cryptanthus*

- Tools (small dowels, terrarium tweezers)

- Decorative rock or gravel (optional)

- Spray bottle with water

How it works

A sealed terrarium receives light and heat from the sun. It should be kept in bright, indirect sunlight. The moisture created within the terrarium evaporates, condenses on the glass, and then drips down the inside of the glass, providing water for the plants. The air trapped inside the sealed terrarium is constantly recycled by the plants, which, to put it simply, use carbon dioxide and light during the day to produce oxygen and food through photosynthesis, and at night use the oxygen to produce carbon dioxide. It is a small, self-sustaining environment. Plants that thrive in a terrarium include ferns, mosses, orchids, and *Philodendron*.

Steps

1. Place a small layer of red lava rock at the bottom of the container (a funnel can be used to guide the rock and soil toward the bottom of the container).
2. Add a small layer of activated charcoal on top of the lava rock.
3. Next, add a layer of soil to the container (approximately 1–2 inches).
4. If you choose to use decorative sand, add it now. If not, add another 1 inch of soil.
5. Decide where you want your plants/moss. Using a small dowel, make a crater to house each plant.
6. Use tweezers to help place the plants into the craters, then gently cover the plants with soil.
7. If you like, add decorative rock or gravel on top of the soil in areas not occupied by plants.
8. Once everything is in place to your liking, use the water bottle to spray the interior sides of the terrarium. This helps to remove debris and gives the terrarium its initial source of water.
9. Seal your terrarium and you're done.

HEMIONITIS ARIFOLIA
HYPOESTES

Pinch pots

These air-dry clay pinch pots are fun, easy, and inexpensive to make. Use them to decorate your own home or give them as a gift to a plant-loving friend. Get creative by adding texture and designs, or leave natural for a more modern look. They can be painted or dressed up with different-colored string. These pinch pots are a perfect way to display your favorite Air Plants.

Before you begin
Set up a work surface with parchment paper. Air-dry clay isn't too messy, but you definitely want to protect your surface from dried-on clay and water stains. Wash your hands to prevent any dirt or oils on your hands from getting into the clay. To make a palm-sized pinch pot, use a 2-inch ball of clay. Allow 24 hours for your pot to dry before painting or hanging it.

TILLANDSIA

Supplies

- Work surface and parchment paper
- Air-dry clay (can be found at craft stores and online)
- Small cup of water
- Chopstick or bamboo skewer
- String, ribbon, or hemp for hanging the pot
- Scissors
- Ruler/tape measure
- *Tillandsia*

Steps

1. Break off a piece of air-dry clay and roll it into a ball between your palms.
2. Hold the ball in one hand and place the opposite thumb in the middle of the ball.
3. With your thumb and forefinger, begin pinching the sides of the clay, turning it as you go.
4. Add tiny splashes of water, when needed, if the clay starts to crack or harden.
5. Continue turning and pinching until you achieve your desired pot shape. Don't make the pot less than ¼ inch thick.
6. Take the bamboo skewer and poke three separate holes, evenly spaced, near the top edge of the pot.
7. Set the pot on parchment paper and allow to dry for 24 hours.
8. Decide the length you want your pot to hang. Measure out three pieces of string. Each one should be twice the length of your desired hanging height (so if you want the pinch pot to hang 12 inches, cut three pieces of string each 24 inches long).
9. Thread each piece of string through a single hole, pull all pieces together at the top and tie together.

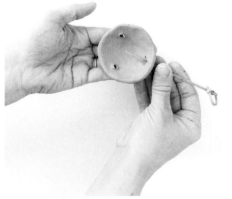

Plant stands

For plants with trailing habits, such as *Peperomia prostrata* or *Senecio rowleyanus*, a plant stand helps to accentuate the beauty of the long foliage strands. Of course, you can make just about anything into a plant stand, from a stack of vintage books to a side table, but if you're like us and you've got that DIY spirit, this project will allow you to have something unique for your home, true to your own style. When finished, doll it up by adding painted stripes to the wooden legs, or even paint the cement to match the decor in your home.

OXALIS TRIANGULARIS

Supplies

- Plastic container (clean and dry, to act as a mold)
- Marker pen
- Cooking-oil spray
- Quick-drying cement powder
- Water
- Empty bowl for mixing
- Stirring stick
- Wooden dowels or copper tubing for legs
- Sandpaper
- High-strength craft glue for use if the legs are loose
- Craft paint and masking tape (if you want to add embellishments)

Before you begin

The bottom of the container you choose as your mold will become the top of your plant stand, so, if you are going for a particular look, choose carefully. For example, if you want a square stand, use a square container. Cardboard containers can work if the perfect shape can't be found in plastic, but plastic produces a smoother finish. Any notches, creases, divots, or words in your container will be visible on your finished product, so look for something smooth.

Before pouring the mixed quick-drying cement into the container, decide how thick you want the top to be. Use a marker pen to create a fill line (we recommend ½–2 inches). Cement is heavy, and so it's important that the thickness of the top should be appropriate for the thickness of the legs; don't make a 2-inch top to be supported by ⅛-inch dowels.

Cut the legs to the desired height. Note that they will be placed about ¼–½ inch into the cement, so build that in if you have a specific height in mind. Many hardware and big-box stores will make cuts for you if you purchase materials from them. Otherwise, find pre-cut dowels at a craft store or cut them at home if you have the necessary equipment.

Also, before you pour, decide where in the container you want to place the legs. You'll need to work fast once you pour because most cement mixes dry fairly fast. Place the legs near the center and equidistant from one another.

A plastic container can be reused after the drying period, so it's easy to make multiples if you have all your materials set up before you start mixing and pouring.

PILEA PEPEROMIOIDES
EPISCIA 'PINK SMOKE'
PELLIONIA PULCHRA
ACANTHOCEREUS TETRAGONUS

Steps

1. Spray the inside of the container with cooking-oil spray and set aside.
2. Mix and stir the cement according to the package directions. Usually, it's a one-to-one ratio of powder to water. Each stand will require a different amount of mixture but should not require the entire bag of cement. Choose a mixing bowl similar in size to the finishing mold so it's easy to judge how much mix to use. Stir and adjust the powder or water level until you achieve a thick, paste-like consistency.
3. Pour or spoon the mixture into the pre-sprayed container up to the fill line. Gently tap/bounce the container on a flat surface to release any air bubbles in the mixture. Any leftover cement can be poured into a plastic bag and thrown away.
4. Insert the legs into the mixture at least ¼ inch, but ideally further. Be careful not to push them through to the full depth of the cement. Arrange the legs so they splay outward. Try to keep them equidistant but don't worry about being perfect. These homemade stands look best when they have some character. You may need to hold the legs in place briefly while the mixture sets.
5. Allow the stand to dry for 24 hours.
6. Invert the stand and lift off the container. The cooking spray should make for easy removal. Use sandpaper to smooth out any imperfections.
7. If the legs feel loose after 24 hours, use heavy-duty glue on the legs and in the holes to set them in place. Put the stand right side up so there is added pressure where the glue contacts both surfaces.
8. To add color to wooden legs, use masking tape wherever you don't want paint and use a brush to add decoration. You can do the same for the cement if it's thick enough for a decorative stripe.

EPISCIA 'PINK SMOKE'
SEMPERVIVUM
ADENIUM
MAMMILLARIA
PEPEROMIA PROSTRATA
DISCHIDIA RUSCIFOLIA

Pegboard

Perfect for small spaces, pegboards keep plants organized and out of reach of pets and children. You can showcase small plants vertically and style them in many different ways. Pegboards can be found online or at your local home-improvement store. They come in different materials including metal, plastic, and fiberboard. Here, we have used fiberboard, which can be purchased in either a natural color or white. They are easily customizable: paint the board any color you like and use the different accessories available to create the perfect look for your home.

Before you begin

The wall frame can be any size you choose, as long as it's not bigger than the pegboard you have. The pegboard will be cut to the same size as the glass in the frame. The glass will be discarded, or you can keep it for some other use. Your pegboard should be big enough for the type of accessories and plants you're using; we suggest 16 x 20 inches or larger. If you plan on painting your pegboard, let the paint dry for at least 24 hours before completing the rest of the project.

Supplies

- Wall picture frame with closure tabs (the metal tabs that close over the back)

- Pegboard

- Pencil

- Handsaw

- Nails

- Pegboard hooks, pegs, and hangers

- Plants (small pots, mounts, cuttings in glass jars, Air Plants, etc.)

Steps

1. Remove all glass and backing from the frame and set aside.
2. Carefully take the glass and set it on top of the pegboard, lining up the holes vertically and horizontally. Outline the glass with a pencil to create the cutting line.
3. Cut the pegboard along the lines with the handsaw and insert the pegboard into the frame. Secure with the frame tabs and hang the framed pegboard on the wall with nails.
4. Attach hooks to the pegboard and start decorating with plants. Pegboard baskets are the perfect place to house small potted plants. Mounted plants will hang nicely on small hooks. Add finishing touches such as botanical artwork or pressed flowers to your pegboard plant display for a personal touch.

Frameless pegboard option

Another option for your pegboard is to forego the frame. You can hang just the pegboard on the wall with one drywall screw through each corner. Use a nut between the wall and the pegboard to create enough space for the hooks behind the pegboard.

HOYA OBOVATA
TILLANDSIA
PHILODENDRON HEDERACEUM 'BRASIL'
TRADESCANTIA FLUMINENSIS 'TRICOLOR'

LIVING
WITH PLANTS

Using botanicals in home decor is both trendy and timeless. Plants can accentuate any interior style, from boho to modern to classic and beyond. Choosing houseplants that match your personal style is easy, since they come in such a variety of shapes, colors, textures, and sizes. Whether you have one plant or many, see how easy it can be to create a green living space.

Stand-alone plant displays

Single plants work well in large spaces where they can be the center of attention. House the plant in a pot that complements your decor colors. For added height, prop the plant up on a plant stand.

Great options for stand-alone plants

· *Monstera deliciosa*

· *Chlorophytum comosum*

· *Ficus elastica*

· *Ficus lyrata*

· *Pellionia repens*

Group plant displays

Outdoor landscapers may be familiar with the plant grouping description of "thrillers, fillers, and spillers." When grouping plants (whether indoors or out), it's a handy reminder of what works well together. Thrillers are the tall plants that stand out among the rest as big and bold. Fillers tend to be less flashy but grow well and are easy to care for. Spillers are cascading plants that overflow the pot. Using all three types to create a plant grouping in your home will bring visual interest to any space.

Hanging plants

Don't limit yourself to windowsills and tabletops: another way to display plants is by hanging them. Plant hangers come in many styles, including beaded, fringed, and tie-dyed, or simple knotted macramé. Plant hangers can be used against a wall or hung directly from the ceiling, depending on your available space and light.

Great options for hanging plants

- *Scindapsus pictus*
- *Epipremnum aureum*
- *Peperomia prostrata*
- *Ceropegia woodii*
- *Chlorophytum comosum*
- *Philodendron hederaceum*
- *Rhipsalis*
- *Hoya*

Fun with containers

Create an instant conversation piece by putting a plant in an unexpected vessel. The ideas are endless, from ferns in coffee cups to succulents in toy dinosaurs. Go glam by hollowing out a hole in a disco ball to fit an existing pot, or create depth by placing a plant inside a bird cage and allowing the foliage to climb up or drape down. Or go tiny with mini cacti and succulents in micro-sized planters for an extra-cute look. Be creative when selecting a fun container but keep drainage in mind. If you can't add a drainage hole to your selected vessel, scale back on watering or use a removable plastic pot for watering time.

Plant shelfies

Plant shelfies are another fun way you can decorate with plants, and they provide great photo opportunities. You can devote as much or as little of the shelf to plants as you like, but we prefer our plant shelfies brimming with botanicals. Cube bookshelves house potted plants exceptionally well—they can be hung on the wall or left free-standing on the floor. Side tables, windowsills, and fireplace mantels also make great spaces for display.

Living the plant life

Some people whose childhood homes were filled with greenery grew up to become green thumbs themselves. Others fell in love with plants later in life by reading decor magazines, watching gardening shows, or following social-media accounts such as House Plant Club. Regardless of how you got here, living the plant life can be a rewarding and lifelong endeavor. Rather than seeing houseplant care as a chore, use it as a time to pause and reflect on life's small wonders. A flower bud on your *Hoya* or a new blade on your Snake Plant can provide great satisfaction when you know that, with your loving care, you're the one who made it happen.

Take it a step farther and share your passion for plants with like-minded people. Check to see if there is a group that meets in your area where you can trade plants or swap cuttings. This is a great way to teach others what you know while learning from those around you. Familiarize yourself with your local plant stores and nurseries. Many will offer outstanding workshops and classes with plant-related activities and DIY.

Try your hand at styling a plant vignette to photograph and share online. Capture your favorite plant hanging in a great vintage macramé find, or snap some succulents on a windowsill. There's a hashtag for everything. Discover what people around the world are doing to raise happy houseplants and how they're incorporating greenery into their lives. Join us and our daily plant inspirations through House Plant Club. Connect with others who have also made the decision to live the plant life.

EPIPREMNUM AUREUM

About the authors

Morgan Doane lives in Tampa, Florida, with her husband, Brian, and their little dog, Foster. She loves String of Pearls (*Senecio rowleyanus*), *Pilea peperomioides*, and *Monstera deliciosa*, and her favorite way to display them is in pots she collects while traveling. When she's not potting, pruning, watering, or photographing her own plant gang, she enjoys visiting botanic gardens and finding inspiration outdoors.

Erin Harding lives in Portland, Oregon, with her husband, Tim, and sons Oliver and Otis. She purchased her first houseplant, the Pregnant Onion Plant (*Ornithogalum longibracteatum*), over 20 years ago, and now shares her home with more than 80 houseplants. Erin loves being home with her boys, teaching them everything, from creating their own Lego planters to mounting *Hoyas*. When she has free time, she enjoys strolling through local plant shops, and dinner dates with Tim.

Acknowledgments

You have to put up with a lot when you live with a plant person writing a book. There's the endless cups of water with propagated plants poking out, the inevitable piles of dirt from terra-cotta accidents, and the tripod waiting to trip you up whenever you walk into a room. For these and many other reasons, we'd like to thank our families first and foremost.

Thank you to Brian Doane for holding up white boards, tending to *Pileas*, and building propagation stations in the middle of the night. To Foster the morkie, thank you for not eating the houseplants. And to Terri Hamrick, thank you for the decades of plant-lady inspiration.

Thank you to Tim Harding for the constant love, support, and comic relief. To Oliver and Otis, thank you for always being there to lend a tiny hand. And thank you to Bob and Memry Walker for always supporting House Plant Club.

Many others contributed to this project in various ways. We'd like to thank the following friends for their knowledge and support. To Amanda Garvin for her photography guidance. To Bryson Mosley for carrying his *Monstera* all over Portland for us. To Cory Paul Jarrell for delivering the car-full of plants. To Gregg Harris at Roosevelt's Terrariums for opening his shop on his day off so that we could have fun playing with dirt. And to Jamie O'Berry for her succulent expertise, thank you. To Caryn Braunstein and Emmanuel Rittner, Kalen Konopka, and Dana Seth Wallace: thank you for inviting us into your homes—we hope we didn't leave any dirt behind!

Many of the plants pictured in this book came from three of our favorite nurseries. Thank you to Justin and all at Costa Farms for providing beautiful houseplants to us in both Tampa and Portland. To Robby and Megan at Fancy Free Nursery and Jesse and Ariana at Pistils Nursery, thank you for opening your shops for us to photograph your amazing greenery.

To Chelsea Edwards and Zara Larcombe and the team at Laurence King Publishing for championing a book about plants and helping us see a dream come to fruition. Thank you. And thank you to Masumi Briozzo for designing such a fun book. We feel very lucky to be able to work with such a great team.

Finally, we'd like to thank the House Plant Club community for raising so many happy houseplants and sharing them with us online. #love, Morgan & Erin.

Costa Farms
Miami, FL
@costafarms

Fancy Free Nursery
Tampa, FL
@fancyfreenursery

House Plant Club
Tampa, FL, & Portland, OR
@houseplantclub

O'Berry's Succulents
St. Petersburg, FL
@oberryssucculents
Pistils Nursery

Portland, OR
@pistilsnursery

Roosevelt's Terrariums
Portland, OR
@rooseveltspdx

The Potted Elephant
Portland, OR
@thepottedelephant